CAN I TRUST
the BIBLE?

The Crucial Questions Series
By R. C. Sproul

CRUCIAL
QUESTIONS
No. | 2

CAN I TRUST
the BIBLE?

R.C. SPROUL

ΙΉ *Reformation Trust* A DIVISION OF LIGONIER MINISTRIES, ORLANDO, FL

Can I Trust the Bible?

© 2009 by R.C. Sproul

Previously published as *Explaining Inerrancy: A Commentary* (1980) by the
International Council on Biblical Inerrancy and as *Explaining Inerrancy* (1996) by
Ligonier Ministries.

Published by Reformation Trust Publishing
a division of Ligonier Ministries
421 Ligonier Court, Sanford, FL 32771
Ligonier.org   ReformationTrust.com

Printed in North Mankato, MN
Corporate Graphics
September 2014
First edition, ninth printing

Cover design: Gearbox Studios
Interior design and typeset: Katherine Lloyd, The DESK

All Scripture quotations are from *The Holy Bible, English Standard Version*®,
copyright © 2001 by Crossway Bibles, a publishing ministry of Good News
Publishers. Used by permission. All rights reserved.

Library of Congress Cataloging-in-Publication Data

Sproul, R. C. (Robert Charles), 1939-

 [Explaining inerrancy]

 Can I trust the Bible? / R.C. Sproul.

  p. cm. -- (The crucial questions series)

 Originally published as: Explaining inerrancy : a commentary by the International
Council on Biblical Inerrancy, 1980 and as Explaining inerrancy by Ligonier
Ministries, 1996.

 ISBN 978-1-56769-182-5

 1. Bible--Evidences, authority, etc. I. Title.

 BS480.S655 2009

 220.1'3--dc22

                        2009018822

Contents

Foreword

The International Council on Biblical Inerrancy was a California-based organization from 1977 to 1987. Its purpose was the defense and application of the doctrine of biblical inerrancy as an essential element for the authority of the church. It was created to counter the drift from this important doctrinal foundation by significant segments of evangelicalism and the outright denial of it by other church movements.

In October 1978, the council held a summit meeting in Chicago. At that time, it issued a statement on biblical inerrancy that included a Preamble, a Short Statement, Nineteen Articles of Affirmation and Denial, and a more ample Exposition. Materials submitted at the meeting had been prepared by Drs. Edmund P. Clowney, James I.

Packer, and R. C. Sproul. These were discussed in a number of ways by groups of delegates from the Advisory Board and in various partial and plenary sessions at the summit. Furthermore, written comments were solicited and received in considerable numbers. A Draft Committee composed of Drs. Clowney, Packer, Sproul, Norman L. Geisler, Harold W. Hoehner, Donald E. Hoke, Roger R. Nicole, and Earl D. Radmacher labored very hard around the clock to prepare a statement that might receive the approval of a great majority of the participants. Very special attention was devoted to the Nineteen Articles of Affirmation and Denial. (The Preamble and the Short Statement were also subjected to editorial revisions. The Exposition was left largely as received.) After considerable discussion, the Draft Committee's submission received a very substantial endorsement by the participants: 240 (out of a total of 268) affixed their signatures to the Nineteen Articles.

It was indicated that the Draft Committee would meet within the year to review and, if necessary, revise the statement. That meeting took place in the fall of 1979, with Drs. Geisler, Hoehner, Nicole, and Radmacher in attendance. It was the consensus of those present that we should not undertake to modify a statement that so many people had signed, both at the summit meeting and afterward. But in order to ward off misunderstandings and to provide an exposition of the position advocated by the ICBI, it was thought desirable to provide a commentary on each of the articles. A draft commentary was prepared by Dr. Sproul and was submitted to the members of the Draft Committee. A number of editorial changes were made, and the final result is what is contained in this booklet.

Dr. Sproul is well qualified to write such a commentary. He had prepared the first draft of the Nineteen Articles, and although they underwent considerable change in the editing process, Dr. Sproul was closely involved in all discussions conducted by the Draft Committee. The present text makes clear exactly what the Council affirmed and denied. Obviously, those who signed the articles do not necessarily concur in every interpretation advocated by the commentary. Not even the members of the Draft Committee are bound by this, and perhaps not even Dr. Sproul, since his text underwent certain editorial revisions. However, this commentary represents an effort at making clear the precise position of the International Council on Biblical Inerrancy as a whole.

In the editing process, we strove to take account of the comments that were forwarded to us. In some cases, we could not concur with those who made comments, and therefore the changes solicited could not be made. In other cases, matters were brought to our notice that in our judgment deserved consideration. We trust that the commentary removes ambiguities and deals effectively with possible misunderstandings.

There is a remarkable unity of views among the members of the Council and the Board, and this should be reflected not only in the articles in their original form but also in the present publication. It was not the aim of those who gathered at Chicago to break relations with those who do not share our convictions concerning the doctrine of Scripture. Rather, the aim was and continues to be to bear witness to what we are convinced is the biblical doctrine on the great subject of the inspiration of Scripture. In making this confession and presenting this commentary, we hope to dispel misunderstandings with which the doctrine of inerrancy has so frequently been burdened and to present with winsomeness and clarity this great tenet in witness to which we are gladly uniting.

—*Roger R. Nicole*

Preface

In the 1970s, Harold Lindsell published a book titled *The Battle for the Bible*. In that little book, Lindsell addressed what had become a huge matter of controversy—the truthfulness and reliability of the Scriptures. In the face of myriad arguments against the inspiration, infallibility, and inerrancy of the Bible, Lindsell took a stand and declared that the Bible remains trustworthy.

It was this same desire to stand against the persistent questioning of the Bible's integrity that brought together more than 250 evangelical leaders in Chicago, Illinois, in October 1978. That summit meeting, convened by the International Council on Biblical Inerrancy, sought to draw a line in the sand, affirming the historic Protestant position on the Scriptures. The result was the Chicago Statement on Biblical Inerrancy.

The issue is crucial. It is via the Scriptures that the church historically has claimed to understand matters of faith and life, from God's creation of all things from nothing to the significance of the life, death, resurrection, and ascension of Jesus Christ to the ultimate consummation of all things toward which history is moving. If the Bible is unreliable in what it teaches about these things, the church is left to speculate and has nothing of value to speak to the world.

In the thirty-plus years since the summit meeting, the battle for the Bible has not abated. It is more crucial than ever that believers understand what the Bible is and why they can trust it wholeheartedly.

This booklet is a brief commentary on the affirmations and denials of the Chicago Statement. While it may seem technical at times, I trust it makes a solid case that the Bible is inerrant in its whole extent.

Ultimately, we believe the Bible to be inerrant because it comes from God Himself. It is unthinkable to contemplate that God might be capable of error. Therefore, His Word cannot possibly contain errors. This is our faith—we can trust the Bible because we can trust God.

—*R. C. Sproul*

THE CHICAGO STATEMENT ON BIBLICAL INERRANCY

The authority of Scripture is a key issue for the Christian church in this and every age. Those who profess faith in Jesus Christ as Lord and Savior are called to show the reality of their discipleship by humbly and faithfully obeying God's written Word. To stray from Scripture in faith or conduct is disloyalty to our Master. Recognition of the total truth and trustworthiness of Holy Scripture is essential to a full grasp and adequate confession of its authority.

The following statement affirms this inerrancy of Scripture afresh, making clear our understanding of it and warning against its denial. We are persuaded that to deny it is to set aside the witness of Jesus Christ and of the Holy Spirit and to refuse that submission to the claims of God's own Word that marks true Christian faith. We see it as our timely duty to make this affirmation in the face of current lapses from the truth of inerrancy among our fellow Christians and misunderstanding of this doctrine in the world at large.

This statement consists of three parts: a Summary Statement, Articles of Affirmation and Denial, and an accompanying Exposition. It has been prepared in the course of a three-day consultation in Chicago. Those who have signed the Summary Statement and the Articles wish to affirm their own conviction as to the inerrancy of Scripture and to encourage and challenge one another and all Christians to growing appreciation and understanding of this doctrine. We acknowledge the limitations of a document prepared in a brief, intensive conference and do not propose that this statement be given creedal weight. Yet we rejoice in the deepening of our own convictions through our discussions together, and we pray that the statement we have signed may be used to the glory of our God toward a new reformation of the church in its faith, life, and mission.

We offer this statement in a spirit, not of contention, but of humility and love, which we purpose by God's grace to maintain in any future dialogue arising out of what we have said. We gladly acknowledge that many who deny the inerrancy of Scripture do not display the consequences of this denial in the rest of their belief and behavior, and we are conscious that we who confess this doctrine often deny it in life by failing to bring our thoughts and deeds, our traditions and habits, into true subjection to the divine Word.

We invite response to this statement from any who see reason to amend its affirmations about Scripture by the light of Scripture itself, under whose infallible authority we stand as we speak. We claim no personal infallibility for the witness we bear, and for any help that enables us to strengthen this testimony to God's Word we shall be grateful.

A SHORT STATEMENT

1. God, who is Himself truth and speaks truth only, has inspired Holy Scripture in order thereby to reveal Himself to lost mankind through Jesus Christ as Creator and Lord, Redeemer and Judge. Holy Scripture is God's witness to Himself.

2. Holy Scripture, being God's own Word, written by men prepared and superintended by His Spirit, is of infallible divine authority in all matters upon which it touches: it is to be believed, as God's instruction, in all that it affirms; obeyed, as God's command, in all that it requires; embraced, as God's pledge, in all that it promises.

3. The Holy Spirit, Scripture's divine author, both authenticates it to us by His inward witness and opens our minds to understand its meaning.

4. Being wholly and verbally God-given, Scripture is without error or fault in all its teaching, no less in what it states about God's acts in creation, about the events of world history, and

about its own literary origins under God, than in its witness to God's saving grace in individual lives.

5. The authority of Scripture is inescapably impaired if this total divine inerrancy is in any way limited or disregarded, or made relative to a view of truth contrary to the Bible's own; and such lapses bring serious loss to both the individual and the church.

ARTICLES OF AFFIRMATION AND DENIAL

Article I

We affirm that the Holy Scriptures are to be received as the authoritative Word of God. **We deny** that the Scriptures receive their authority from the church, tradition, or any other human source.

Article II

We affirm that the Scriptures are the supreme written norm by which God binds the conscience, and that the authority of the church is subordinate to that of Scripture. **We deny** that church creeds, councils, or declarations have authority greater than or equal to the authority of the Bible.

Article III

We affirm that the written Word in its entirety is revelation given by God. **We deny** that the Bible is merely a witness to revelation, or only becomes revelation in encounter, or depends on the responses of men for its validity.

Article IV

We affirm that God who made mankind in His image has used language as a means of revelation. **We deny** that human language is so limited by our creatureliness that it is rendered inadequate as a vehicle for divine revelation. We further deny that the corruption of human culture and language through sin has thwarted God's work of inspiration.

Article V

We affirm that God's revelation within the Holy Scriptures was progressive. **We deny** that later revelation, which may fulfill earlier revelation, ever corrects or contradicts it. We further deny that any normative revelation has been given since the completion of the New Testament writings.

Article VI

We affirm that the whole of Scripture and all its parts, down to the very words of the original, were given by divine inspiration. **We deny** that the inspiration of Scripture can rightly be affirmed of the whole without the parts, or of some parts but not the whole.

Article VII

We affirm that inspiration was the work in which God by His Spirit, through human writers, gave us His Word. The origin of Scripture is divine. The mode of divine inspiration remains largely a mystery to us. **We deny** that inspiration can be reduced to human insight, or to heightened states of consciousness of any kind.

Article VIII

We affirm that God in His work of inspiration utilized the distinctive personalities and literary styles of the writers whom He had chosen and prepared. **We deny** that God, in causing these writers to use the very words that He chose, overrode their personalities.

Article IX

We affirm that inspiration, though not conferring omniscience, guaranteed true and trustworthy utterance on all matters of which the biblical authors were moved to speak and write. **We deny** that the finitude or fallenness of these writers, by necessity or otherwise, introduced distortion or falsehood into God's Word.

Article X

We affirm that inspiration, strictly speaking, applies only to the autographic text of Scripture, which in the providence of God can be ascertained from available manuscripts with great accuracy. We further affirm that copies and translations of Scripture are the Word of God to the extent that they faithfully represent the original. **We deny** that any essential element of the Christian faith is affected by the absence of the autographs. We further deny that this absence renders the assertion of biblical inerrancy invalid or irrelevant.

Article XI

We affirm that Scripture, having been given by divine inspiration, is infallible, so that, far from misleading us, it is true and reliable in all the matters it addresses. **We deny** that it is possible for the Bible to be at the same time infallible and errant in its assertions. Infallibility and inerrancy may be distinguished, but not separated.

Article XII

We affirm that Scripture in its entirety is inerrant, being free from all falsehood, fraud, or deceit. **We deny** that biblical infallibility and inerrancy are limited to spiritual, religious, or redemptive themes, exclusive of assertions in the fields of history and science. We further deny that scientific hypotheses about earth history may properly be used to overturn the teaching of Scripture on creation and the flood.

Article XIII

We affirm the propriety of using inerrancy as a theological term with reference to the complete truthfulness of Scripture. **We deny** that it is proper to evaluate Scripture according to standards of truth and error that are alien to its usage or purpose. We further deny that inerrancy is negated by biblical phenomena such as a lack of modern technical precision, irregularities of grammar or spelling, observational descriptions of nature, the reporting of falsehoods, the use of hyperbole and round numbers, the topical arrangement of material, variant selections of material in parallel accounts, or the use of free citations.

Article XIV

We affirm the unity and internal consistency of Scripture.

We deny that alleged errors and discrepancies that have not yet been resolved vitiate the truth claims of the Bible.

Article XV
We affirm that the doctrine of inerrancy is grounded in the teaching of the Bible about inspiration. **We deny** that Jesus' teaching about Scripture may be dismissed by appeals to accommodation or to any natural limitation of His humanity.

Article XVI
We affirm that the doctrine of inerrancy has been integral to the church's faith throughout its history. **We deny** that inerrancy is a doctrine invented by scholastic Protestantism, or is a reactionary position postulated in response to negative higher criticism.

Article XVII
We affirm that the Holy Spirit bears witness to the Scriptures, assuring believers of the truthfulness of God's written Word. **We deny** that this witness of the Holy Spirit operates in isolation from or against Scripture.

Article XVIII
We affirm that the text of Scripture is to be interpreted by grammatico-historical exegesis, taking account of its literary forms and devices, and that Scripture is to interpret Scripture. **We deny** the legitimacy of any treatment of the text or quest for sources lying behind it that leads to relativizing, dehistoricizing, or discounting its teaching, or rejecting its claims to authorship.

Article XIX

We affirm that a confession of the full authority, infallibility, and inerrancy of Scripture is vital to a sound understanding of the whole of the Christian faith. We further affirm that such confession should lead to increasing conformity to the image of Christ. **We deny** that such confession is necessary for salvation. However, we further deny that inerrancy can be rejected without grave consequences, both to the individual and to the church.

EXPOSITION

Our understanding of the doctrine of inerrancy must be set in the context of the broader teachings of Scripture concerning itself. This exposition gives an account of the outline of doctrine from which our summary statement and articles are drawn.

Creation, Revelation, and Inspiration

The triune God, who formed all things by His creative utterances and governs all things by His word of decree, made mankind in His own image for a life of communion with Himself, on the model of the eternal fellowship of loving communication within the Godhead. As God's image-bearer, man was to hear God's Word addressed to him and to respond in the joy of adoring obedience. Over and above God's self-disclosure in the created order and the sequence of events within it, human beings from Adam on have received verbal messages from Him, either directly, as stated in Scripture, or indirectly in the form of part or all of Scripture itself.

When Adam fell, the Creator did not abandon mankind to final judgment but promised salvation and began to reveal Himself as Redeemer in a sequence of historical events centering on Abraham's family and culminating in the life, death, resurrection, present heavenly ministry, and promised return of Jesus Christ. Within this frame God has from time to time spoken specific words of judgment and mercy, promise and command, to sinful human beings, so drawing them into a covenant relation of mutual commitment between Him and them in which He blesses them with gifts of grace and they bless Him in responsive adoration. Moses, whom God used as mediator to carry His words to His people at the time of the Exodus, stands at the head of a long line of prophets in whose mouths and writings God put His words for delivery to Israel. God's purpose in this succession of messages was to maintain His covenant by causing His people to know His name—that is, His nature—and His will both of precept and purpose in the present and for the future. This line of prophetic spokesmen from God came to completion in Jesus Christ, God's incarnate Word, who was Himself a prophet—more than a prophet, but not less—and in the apostles and prophets of the first Christian generation. When God's final and climactic message, His Word to the world concerning Jesus Christ, had been spoken and elucidated by those in the apostolic circle, the sequence of revealed messages ceased. Henceforth, the church was to live and know God by what He had already said, and said for all time.

At Sinai, God wrote the terms of His covenant on tables of stone, as His enduring witness and for lasting accessibility, and throughout the period of prophetic and apostolic revelation He prompted men to write the messages given to and through them, along with celebratory records of His dealings with His people, plus moral reflections on covenant life and forms of praise and prayer for covenant mercy. The theological reality of inspiration in the producing of biblical documents corresponds to that of spoken prophecies: although the human writers' personalities were expressed in what they wrote, the words were divinely constituted. Thus, what Scripture says, God says; its authority is His authority, for He is its ultimate Author, having given it through the minds and words of chosen and prepared men who in freedom and faithfulness "spoke from God as they were carried along by the Holy Spirit" (2 Peter 1:21). Holy Scripture must be acknowledged as the Word of God by virtue of its divine origin.

Authority: Christ and the Bible

Jesus Christ, the Son of God who is the Word made flesh, our Prophet, Priest, and King, is the ultimate Mediator of God's communication to man, as He is of all God's gifts of grace. The revelation He gave was more than verbal; He revealed the Father by His presence and His deeds as well. Yet His words were crucially important; for He was God, He spoke from the Father, and His words will judge all men at the last day.

As the prophesied Messiah, Jesus Christ is the central theme of Scripture. The Old Testament looked ahead to Him; the New Testament looks back to His first coming and on to His second. Canonical Scripture is the divinely inspired and therefore normative witness to Christ. No hermeneutic, therefore, of which the historical Christ is not the focal point is acceptable. Holy Scripture must be treated as what it essentially is—the witness of the Father to the incarnate Son.

It appears that the Old Testament canon had been fixed by the time of Jesus. The New Testament canon is likewise now closed inasmuch as no new apostolic witness to the historical Christ can now be borne. No new revelation (as distinct from Spirit-given understanding of existing revelation) will be given until Christ comes again. The canon was created in principle by divine inspiration. The church's part was to discern the canon that God had created, not to devise one of its own.

The word canon, signifying a rule or standard, is a pointer to authority, which means the right to rule and control. Authority in Christianity belongs to God in His revelation, which means, on the one hand, Jesus Christ, the living Word, and, on the other hand, Holy Scripture, the written Word. The authority of Christ and that of Scripture are one. As our Prophet, Christ testified that Scripture cannot be broken. As our Priest and King, He devoted His earthly life to fulfilling the Law and the Prophets, even dying in obedience to the words of messianic prophecy. Thus, as He saw Scripture attesting Him and His authority, so by His own submission to Scripture He attested its authority. As He bowed to

His Father's instruction given in His Bible (our Old Testament), so He requires His disciples to do—not, however, in isolation but in conjunction with the apostolic witness to Himself which He undertook to inspire by His gift of the Holy Spirit. So Christians show themselves faithful servants of their Lord by bowing to the divine instruction given in the prophetic and apostolic writings that together make up our Bible.

By authenticating each other's authority, Christ and Scripture coalesce into a single fount of authority. The biblically interpreted Christ and the Christ-centered, Christ-proclaiming Bible are from this standpoint one. As from the fact of inspiration we infer that what Scripture says, God says, so from the revealed relation between Jesus Christ and Scripture we may equally declare that what Scripture says, Christ says.

Infallibility, Inerrancy, Interpretation

Holy Scripture, as the inspired Word of God witnessing authoritatively to Jesus Christ, may properly be called infallible and inerrant. These negative terms have a special value, for they explicitly safeguard crucial positive truths.

Infallible signifies the quality of neither misleading nor being misled, and so safeguards in categorical terms the truth that Holy Scripture is a sure, safe, and reliable rule and guide in all matters.

Similarly, inerrant signifies the quality of being free from all falsehood or mistake, and so safeguards the truth that Holy Scripture is entirely true and trustworthy in all its assertions.

We affirm that canonical Scripture should always be interpreted on the basis that it is infallible and inerrant. However, in determining what the God-taught writer is asserting in each passage, we must pay the most careful attention to its claims and character as a human production. In inspiration, God utilized the culture and conventions of His penman's milieu, a milieu that God controls in His sovereign providence; it is misinterpretation to imagine otherwise.

So history must be treated as history, poetry as poetry, hyperbole and metaphor as hyperbole and metaphor, generalization and approximation as what they are, and so forth. Differences between literary conventions in Bible times and in ours must also be observed: since, for instance, nonchronological narration and imprecise citation were conventional and acceptable and violated no expectations in those days, we must not regard these things as faults when we find them in Bible writers. When total precision of a particular kind was not expected nor aimed at, it is no error not to have achieved it. Scripture is inerrant, not in the sense of being absolutely precise by modern standards, but in the sense of making good its claims and achieving that measure of focused truth at which its authors aimed.

The truthfulness of Scripture is not negated by the appearance in it of irregularities of grammar or spelling, phenomenal descriptions of nature, reports of false statements (e.g., the lies of Satan), or seeming discrepancies between one passage and another. It is not right to set the so-called "phenomena" of Scripture against the teaching of Scripture about itself. Apparent inconsistencies should not be ignored. Solution of them, where this can be convincingly achieved, will encourage our faith, and where for the present no convincing solution is at hand we shall significantly honor God by trusting His assurance that His Word is true despite these appearances, and by maintaining our confidence that one day they will be seen to have been illusions.

Inasmuch as all Scripture is the product of a single divine mind, interpretation must stay within the bounds of the analogy of Scripture and eschew hypotheses that would correct one biblical passage by another, whether in the name of progressive revelation or of the imperfect enlightenment of the inspired writer's mind.

Although Holy Scripture is nowhere culture-bound in the sense that its teaching lacks universal validity, it is sometimes culturally conditioned by the customs and conventional views of a particular period, so that the application of its principles today calls for a different sort of action.

Skepticism and Criticism

Since the Renaissance, and more particularly since the Enlightenment, worldviews have been developed that involve skepticism about basic Christian tenets. Such are the agnosticism that denies God is knowable, the rationalism that denies He is incomprehensible, the idealism that denies He is transcendent, and the existentialism that denies rationality in His relationships with us.

When these un- and antibiblical principles seep into men's theologies at a presuppositional level, as today they frequently do, faithful interpretation of Holy Scripture becomes impossible.

Transmission and Translation

Since God has nowhere promised an inerrant transmission of Scripture, it is necessary to affirm that only the autographic text of the original documents was inspired and to maintain the need of textual criticism as a means of detecting any slips that may have crept into the text in the course of its transmission. The verdict of this science, however, is that the Hebrew and Greek text appear to be amazingly well preserved, so that we are amply justified in affirming, with the Westminster Confession, a singular providence of God in this matter and in declaring that the authority of Scripture is in no way jeopardized by the fact that the copies we possess are not entirely error free.

Similarly, no translation is or can be perfect, and all translations are an additional step away from the autographa. Yet the verdict of linguistic science is that English-speaking Christians, at least, are exceedingly well served in these days with a host of excellent translations and have no cause for hesitating to conclude that the true Word of God is within their reach. Indeed, in view of the frequent repetition in Scripture of the main matters with which it deals and also of the Holy Spirit's constant witness to and through the Word, no serious translation of Holy Scripture will so destroy its meaning as to render it unable to make its reader "wise for salvation through faith in Christ Jesus" (2 Tim. 3:15).

Inerrancy and Authority

In our affirmation of the authority of Scripture as involving its total truth, we are consciously standing with Christ and His apostles, indeed with the whole Bible and with the mainstream of church history from the first days until very recently. We are concerned at the casual, inadvertent, and seemingly thoughtless way in which a belief of such far-reaching importance has been given up by so many in our day.

We are conscious, too, that great and grave confusion results from ceasing to maintain the total truth of the Bible whose authority one professes to acknowledge. The result of taking this step is that the Bible that God gave loses its authority, and what has authority instead is a Bible reduced in content according to the demands of one's critical reasonings and in principle reducible still further once one has started. This means that at bottom, independent reason now has authority, as opposed to scriptural teaching. If this is not seen and if for the time being basic evangelical doctrines are still held, persons denying the full truth of Scripture may claim an evangelical identity while methodologically they have moved away from the evangelical principle of knowledge to an unstable subjectivism, and will find it hard not to move farther.

We affirm that what Scripture says, God says. May He be glorified. Amen and Amen.

Chapter One

THE BIBLE AND AUTHORITY

The Chicago Statement on Biblical Inerrancy rightly affirms that "the authority of Scripture is a key issue for the Christian church in this and every age." But authority cannot stand in isolation, as the statement shows. The authority of the Bible is based on the fact that it is the written Word of God. Because the Bible is the Word of God and because the God of the Bible is truth and speaks truthfully, the Bible's authority is linked to inerrancy. If the Bible is the Word of God and if God is a God of truth, then the

Bible *must* be inerrant—not merely in some of its parts, as some modern theologians are saying, but totally, as the church for the most part has said down through the ages of its history.

Some of the terms used in the debate about the authority and inerrancy of the Bible are technical ones. Some show up in the Chicago Statement, but they are not difficult to come to understand. They can be mastered (and the doctrine of inerrancy more fully understood) by a little reading and study. This commentary on the Chicago Statement attempts to provide such material in reference to the Nineteen Articles of Affirmation and Denial, which form the heart of the document. The full text of the statement appears as an appendix.

ARTICLE I: Authority

*We **affirm** that the Holy Scriptures are to be received as the authoritative Word of God. **We deny** that the Scriptures receive their authority from the church, tradition, or any other human source.*

The initial article of the Chicago Statement is designed to establish the degree of authority that is to be attributed to the Bible. This article, as well as Article II, makes the statement clearly a Protestant one. Though the Roman Catholic Church consistently and historically has maintained a high view of the inspiration of Holy Scripture, there remains the unresolved problem of the uniqueness and sufficiency of biblical authority for the church.

Rome has placed the traditions of the church alongside Scripture as a supplement to Scripture and, consequently, a source of special revelation beyond the scope of Scripture.

The Roman Catholic Church has asserted continuously that since the church established the extent and scope of the New Testament and Old Testament canon, there is a certain sense in which the authority of the Bible is subordinate to and dependent on the church's approval. These issues of the relationship of church and canon and of the question of multiple sources of special revelation are particularly in view in Articles I and II.

In early drafts of Article I, the extent of the canon was spelled out to include the sixty-six canonical books that are found and embraced within the context of most Protestant-sanctioned editions of the Bible. In discussions among the participants at the summit and because of requests to the Draft Committee, there was considerable sentiment for striking the words "sixty-six canonical books" from the early drafts. This was due to some variance within Christendom as to the exact number of books that are to be recognized within the canon. For example, the Ethiopic Church has included more books in the canon than sixty-six. The final draft affirms simply that the Holy Scriptures are to be received as the authoritative Word of God. For the vast majority of Protestants, the designation "Holy Scripture" has clear reference to the sixty-six canonical books, but it leaves room for those who differ on the canon question to participate in the confession of the nature of Scripture. The specific question of the number of books contained in that canon is left open in this statement.

The question of the scope of the canon, or the list of books that make up our Bible, may confuse many people, particularly those who are accustomed to a number of books clearly defined by their particular church confessions. Some have argued that if one questions a particular book's canonicity, the implication is that one does not believe in a divinely inspired Bible. Perhaps the clearest illustration of this in history comes from the life of Martin Luther, who, at one point in his ministry, had strong reservations about including the book of James in the New Testament canon. Though it is abundantly clear that Luther believed in an inspired Bible, he had questions about whether a particular book should be included in that inspired Bible. Several scholars have tried to use Luther's questioning of the book of James to deny that he believed in inspiration. It is very important to see the difference between the question of the scope of the canon and the question of the inspiration of the books that are recognized as included in the canon. In other words, the nature of Scripture and the extent of Scripture are different questions that must not be confused.

A key word in the affirmation section of Article I is *received*. The initial draft mentioned that the Scriptures are to be received by the church. The phrase "by the church" was deleted because it is clear that the Word of God in Holy Scripture is to be received not only by the church but by everyone. The word *received* has historical significance. In the church councils that considered the canon question, the Latin word *recipimus* ("we receive") was used; the councils were saying "we receive" various books to be included in the canon. By that usage of the word *receive*, the church made clear that it was not declaring certain books to be authoritative by its own authority, but that it was simply acknowledging the Word of God to be the Word of God. By using the word *receive*, the church fathers displayed their willingness to submit to what they regarded to be already the Word of God. Consequently, any notion that the church creates the Bible or is superior to the Bible is denied by those who spelled out the canon.

If any ambiguity about the relationship of Scripture to the church remains in the affirmation, it is removed in the subsequent denial: The Scriptures receive their authority from God, not from the church or from any other human source.

ARTICLE II: Scripture and Tradition

We affirm that the Scriptures are the supreme written norm by which God binds the conscience, and that the authority of the church is subordinate to that of Scripture. We deny that church creeds, councils, or declarations have authority greater than or equal to the authority of the Bible.

Article II of the Chicago Statement reinforces Article I and goes into more detail concerning the matters it addresses. Article II has in view the classical Protestant principle of *sola Scriptura,* which speaks of the unique authority of the Bible to bind the consciences of men. The affirmation of Article II speaks of the Scriptures as "the supreme written norm." At the summit, there was lengthy discussion concerning the word *supreme*; alternative words, such as *ultimate* and *only*, were suggested and subsequently eliminated from the text. The question had to do with the fact that other written documents are important to the life of the church. For example, church creeds and confessions form the basis of subscription and unity of faith in many different Christian denominations and communities. Such creeds and confessions have a kind of normative authority within a given Christian body and have the effect of binding consciences within that particular context. However, it is a classic tenet of Protestants to recognize that all such creeds and confessions are fallible and cannot fully and finally bind the conscience of an individual believer. Only the Word of God has the kind of authority that can bind the consciences of men forever. So while the articles acknowledge that there are other written norms recognized by different bodies of Christians, insofar as they are true, those written norms are derived from and are subordinate to the supreme written norm that is Holy Scripture.

The denial clearly spells out that no church creed, council, or declaration has authority greater than or equal to that of the Bible. Again, any idea that tradition or church officers have authority equal to Scripture is repudiated by this statement. The question of a Christian's obedience to authority structures apart from Scripture was a matter of great discussion with regard to this article. For example, the Bible itself exhorts us to obey the civil magistrates. We are certainly willing to subject ourselves to our own church confessions and to the authority structures of our ecclesiastical bodies. But the thrust of this article is to indicate that whatever lesser authorities may exist, they never carry the authority of God Himself. There is a sense in which all authority in this world is derived from and dependent on the authority of God. God and God alone has intrinsic authority. That intrinsic authority is given to the Bible, since it is God's Word.

Various Christian bodies have defined the extent of civil authority and ecclesiastical authority in different ways. For example, in Reformed churches, the authority of the church is viewed as ministerial and declarative rather than ultimate and intrinsic. God and God alone has the absolute right to bind the consciences of men. Our consciences are justly bound to lesser authorities only when they are in conformity to the Word of God.

Chapter Two

THE BIBLE AND
REVELATION

The next three articles of the Chicago Statement deal with revelation. Article III defines what we mean when we say that the Bible *is* revelation and not merely a *witness to* revelation, as claimed by neoorthodox theologians. Article IV considers the use of human language as a vehicle for divine revelation. Article V notes the way in which the revelation of God unfolds progressively throughout Scripture so that later texts more fully expound the earlier ones. In these articles, the framers of the statement sought to guard against any view that would lessen the unique nature of the Bible as God's written revelation or negate the teaching of some parts of it by appeal to other parts.

ARTICLE III: Revelation

We affirm *that the written Word in its entirety is revelation given by God.* **We deny** *that the Bible is merely a witness to revelation, or only becomes revelation in encounter, or depends on the responses of men for its validity.*

Both the affirmation and denial of Article III deal with the controversial question of the objective character of divine revelation in Scripture. There was considerable debate in the twentieth century on this issue, particularly with the rise of so-called dialectical or neoorthodox theology. This approach sought to promote a "dynamic" view of the Bible that sees the authority of Scripture functioning in a dynamic relationship of Word and hearing of the Word. Several theologians have denied that the Bible, in and of itself, is objective revelation. They maintain that revelation does not occur until there is an inward, subjective human response to that Word. Scholars such as Emil Brunner, for example, have insisted that the Bible is not itself revelation, but is merely a witness to the revelation that is found in Christ. It has become fashionable in certain quarters to maintain that special revelation is embodied in Christ alone, and that to consider the Bible as objective revelation would be to detract from the uniqueness of the person of Christ, the Word made flesh.

The spirit of these articles is to oppose a disjunction between the revelation that is given to us in the person of Christ objectively and the revelation that comes to us in equally objective terms in the Word of God inscripturated. Here the Bible is seen not merely as a catalyst for revelation but as revelation itself. If the Bible is God's Word and its content proceeds from Him, then its content is to be seen as revelation. Here revelation is viewed as "propositional." It is propositional not because the Bible is written in the style of logical equations or analytical formulas. It is propositional because it communicates truth that may be understood as propositions.

In the affirmation of Article III, the words "in its entirety" are significant. There are those who have claimed that the Bible contains revelation from God here and there, in specified places, but that it is the task of the believer individually or the church corporately to separate the parts of Scripture that are revelatory from those that are not. By implication, this article repudiates such an approach to Scripture by affirming that the whole of Scripture, its entire contents, is to be seen as divine revelation.

The denial of Article III reinforces the objectivity of revelation in Scripture and maintains that the validity of this revelation does not rely on human responses. The Bible's truth does not depend in any way on whether a person believes the truth.

The central thrust of Article III is to declare with confidence that the content of Scripture is not the result of human imagination or cleverly devised philosophical opinions, but that it reflects God's sovereign disclosure about Himself and all matters that are touched on by Scripture. The Bible, then, embodies truth that comes to us from beyond the scope of our own abilities. It comes from God Himself.

ARTICLE IV: Human Language

We affirm that God who made mankind in His image has used language as a means of revelation. We deny that human language is so limited by our creatureliness that it is rendered inadequate as a vehicle for divine revelation. We further deny that the corruption of human culture and language through sin has thwarted God's work of inspiration.

One of the most significant attacks on biblical inerrancy in the twentieth century was based on the limitations of human language. Since the Bible was written by human writers, the question emerged again and again whether such human involvement, by virtue of the limitations of human creatureliness, would not, of necessity, render the Bible less than infallible. Since men are not infallible in and of themselves and are prone to error in all that they do, does it not follow logically that anything coming from the pen of man must be errant? To this we reply that errancy is not an inevitable concomitant of human nature. Before the fall, Adam may well have been free from proneness to error, and Christ, though fully human, never erred. Since the fall, it is a common tendency of men to err. We deny, however, that it is necessary for men to err always and everywhere in what they say or write, even apart from inspiration.

Because of divine inspiration and the superintendence of the Holy Spirit in the giving of sacred Scripture, the writings of the Bible are free from the normal tendencies and propensities of fallen men to distort the truth. Though our language, and especially our language about God, is never comprehensive and exhaustive in its ability to capture eternal truths, nevertheless it is adequate to give us truth without falsehood. For example, if we made a statement that Chicago is a city in the state of Illinois, the truth communicated by that statement would in no way be exhaustive. That is, all that could possibly be understood of the nature and scope of the city of Chicago or the complexities of the state of Illinois would not be known by any human being who made such a statement. By contrast, if God made the statement, "Chicago is a city in the state of Illinois," within His mind there would be total comprehension of all that is involved in Chicago and Illinois. Nevertheless, the fact that God made the statement "Chicago is a city in the state of Illinois" would not in itself make the statement more or less true than if a human being made the statement. Though we recognize that human language is limited by creatureliness, we do not allow the inference that human language must necessarily be distortive of truth.

If human language were to be judged intrinsically inadequate to convey revelation, there would be no possible means by which God could reveal anything about Himself to us in verbal form. However, since the Bible teaches that man is created in the image of God and that there is some point of likeness between man and God, communication between God and man is possible. The possibility of such communication is built into creation by God Himself.

With respect to the assertion that human language is so limited that it is inadequate to convey revelation, particularly in view of the effects of sin on our human culture and language, we must say that though man's fall renders us guilty before the divine bar of judgment and though all men are liars (Ps. 116:11), it does not follow necessarily that all men lie all the time. Though all of us lie at one time or another, this does not mean that we lie every time we speak. The human tendency toward corruption and falsehood is precisely that which we believe to be overcome by the divine inspiration and involvement in the preparation of Holy Scripture. Thus, we think that skepticism about biblical integrity based on inferences drawn from the adequacy or inadequacy of human speech is unwarranted.

ARTICLE V: Progressive Revelation

We affirm that God's revelation in the Holy Scriptures was progressive. *We deny* that later revelation, which may fulfill earlier revelation, ever corrects or contradicts *it. We further deny that any normative revelation has been given since the completion of the New Testament writings.*

The issues in view in Article V are of profound importance to the life of the church and are very complicated at times. The affirmation is simply a recognition that within the Bible itself there is a progressive revelation. All that has been revealed of God in the totality of Scripture is not found, for example, in the book of Genesis. Much of the content of God's redemptive activity in Christ is hinted at in part and addressed in shadowy ways in the earlier portions of the Old Testament. But throughout sacred Scripture, the content of divine revelation is expanded, ultimately to the fullness reached in the New Testament. That is what is meant by progressive revelation in this context—that the revelation within Scripture unfolds in an ever-deepening and broadening way.

The denial makes clear that such progress and expansion of revelation does not deny or contradict what was given earlier. Though certain precepts that were obligatory to people in the Old Testament period are no longer so in the New Testament, this does not mean that they were discontinued because they were wicked in the past and God corrected what He formerly endorsed, but rather that certain practices were superseded by newer practices that were consistent with fulfillment of Old Testament activities. This in no way suggests that the Old Testament is irrelevant to the New Testament believer or that earlier revelation may be dismissed out of hand in light of newer revelation. The Bible is to be regarded as a holistic book in which the Old Testament helps us understand the New Testament and the New Testament sheds significant light on the Old Testament. Although progressive revelation is recognized, it is not to be viewed as a license to play loosely with portions of Scripture, setting one dimension of revelation against another within the Bible itself. The Bible's coherency and consistency is not vitiated by progressive revelation within it.

The secondary denial states that no normative revelation has been given to the church since the close of the New Testament canon. This does not mean that God the Holy Spirit has stopped working or that He does not lead His people today. Part of the difficulty is that theological words are used in different ways within different Christian communities. For example, what one group may call "revelation," another group may define as "illumination." Thus, the qualifying word *normative* is important to understanding the secondary denial. It means that no revelation has been given since the first century that merits inclusion in the canon of Holy Scripture. Private leadings or guidance—or "revelations," as some may term them—may not be seen as having the force or authority of Holy Scripture.

Chapter Three

THE BIBLE AND INSPIRATION

Inspiration is the way in which God gave His Word to us through human authors, but how He did this is not fully understood. In this section, the framers of the Articles of Affirmation and Denial explicitly deny understanding the mode of inspiration. But they affirm, as Scripture itself also does (2 Tim. 3:16), that the Bible is the product of divine inspiration and that God's work extended through the human writers to each section and even each word of the original documents. The process of inspiration did not make the biblical writers automatons, for their books reveal differences of vocabulary, style, and other matters. However, inspiration did overcome any tendency they may have had to err, with the result that the words they wrote were precisely what God, the divine Author, intended us to have.

ARTICLE VI: Verbal Plenary Inspiration

We affirm that the whole of Scripture and all its parts, down to the very words of the original, were given by divine inspiration. We deny that the inspiration of Scripture can rightly be affirmed of the whole without the parts, or of some parts but not the whole.

Article VI addresses the doctrine of verbal plenary inspiration. "Plenary" inspiration means that the whole of Scripture is given by divine inspiration. Because some have maintained that the whole has been given by inspiration but some parts of that whole are not of divine inspiration, we are speaking of the origin of Scripture—which does not begin with the insights of men but comes from God Himself.

In the affirmative of Article VI, we read the phrase "down to the very words of the original." The clause "down to the very words" refers to the extent of inspiration, and the words "of the original" indicate that it is the "auto-graphs" that were inspired. The limiting of inspiration to the autographs is covered more fully in Article X, though it is plain in this article that the verbal inspiration of the Bible refers to the original manuscripts.

The fact that Article VI speaks of divine inspiration down to the very words of the original may conjure up in some people's minds the notion that God dictated the words of Scripture. The doctrine of verbal plenary inspiration has often been said to carry the implication of a dictation theory of inspiration. No such theory is spelled out in this article, nor is it implied. In fact, in Article VII, the framers of the statement deny the dictation theory.

The issue of dictation has raised problems in church history. At the Council of Trent in the sixteenth century, the Roman Catholic Church used the word *dictante*, meaning "dictating," with respect to the Spirit's work in the giving of the ancient texts. In the Protestant camp, John Calvin spoke of the biblical writers as being *amanuenses* or secretaries. Added to this is the fact that some portions of Scripture seem to have been given by some form of dictation, such as the Ten Commandments.

In the modern era, dictation cancels out human lit-erary styles, vocabulary choices, and the like. This article does not mean to imply such a method of inspiration that would negate or vitiate the literary styles of the individual authors of the biblical documents. The sense in which Calvin, for example, spoke of secretaries and even in which Trent spoke of dictating could hardly be construed to conform to modern methods of dictating using sophisticated equipment and methods. The context in which these words were used in the past had specific reference to the fact that inspiration shows some analogy to a man issuing a message that is put together by a secretary. The analogy points to the question of origin of the message. In the doctrine of inspiration, what is at stake is the truth that the message is from God rather than from human beings.

The Chicago Statement leaves the mode of inspiration as a mystery (cf. Article VII). Inspiration, as used here, involves a divine superintendence that preserved the writers from using words that would have falsified or distorted the message of Scripture. Thus, on the one hand, the statement affirms that God's superintendence and inspiration of the Bible applied down to the very words and, on the other hand, denies that He canceled out the influence of the writers' personalities in their choices of words used to express the truth revealed.

Evangelical Christians avoid the notion that the biblical writers were passive instruments like pens in the hands of God, yet at the same time they affirm that the net result of the process of inspiration was the same. Calvin, for example, says that we should read the Bible *as if* we have heard God audibly speaking its message. That is, it carries the same weight of authority as if God Himself were giving utterance to the words (*Institutes of the Christian Religion*, 1.7.1). This does not mean that Calvin believed or taught that God did in fact utter the words audibly. We do not know the process by which inspired Scripture was given. But because of inspiration, no matter how God brought it about, every word of Scripture carries the weight of God's authority.

ARTICLE VII: Inspiration

*We **affirm** that inspiration was the work in which God by His Spirit, through human writers, gave us His Word. The origin of Scripture is divine. The mode of divine inspiration remains largely a mystery to us. We **deny** that inspiration can be reduced to human insight or to heightened states of consciousness of any kind.*

Article VII spells out in more detail what is implied in Article VI. Here, clear reference is made to the human writers of the text. The human writers are identified as the instruments by which God's Word comes to us. Classically, the Holy Scriptures have been called the *Verbum Dei*, the Word of God, or even the *vox Dei*, the voice of God. Yet, at the same time, Holy Scripture comes to us as the words of men. In other words, there is an agency of humanity through which God's divine Word is communicated, but the origin of Scripture is divine.

The framers of the document have in view here the primary meaning of the word *theopneustos* in 2 Timothy 3:16, the word often translated "inspired by God." *Theopneustos* literally means "God-breathed"; it has primary reference to God's breathing out His Word rather than breathing some kind of effect into the human writers. So *expiration* is a more accurate term than *inspiration* with respect to the origin of Scripture. But we use the term *inspiration* to cover the whole process by which the Word comes to us. Initially, it comes from the mouth of God (speaking, of course, metaphorically). From its origin in God, it is transmitted through the agency of human writers under divine supervision and superintendence. The next step in the process of communication is the apprehension of the divine message by human beings. This article explicitly states that the precise mode by which God accomplishes inspiration remains a mystery. The document makes no attempt to define the "how" of divine inspiration or even to suggest that the method is known to us.

The word *inspiration* can be used and has been used in

the English language to refer to moments of genius-level insight, of intensified states of consciousness, or of heightened acts of human achievement. We speak of inspired poetry, meaning that the author achieved extraordinary levels of insight and brilliance. However, in this dimension of "inspiration," there is no suggestion that the source of inspiration is divine power. There are human levels of inspiration reflected in heroic acts, brilliant insights, and intensified states of consciousness. But these are not what is meant by the use of *inspiration* as a theological term. Here the Chicago Statement is making clear that something transcending all human states of inspiration is in view, something in which the power and supervision of God are at work. Thus, the articles are saying that the Bible, though it is a human book insofar as it was written by human writers, has its humanity transcended by virtue of its divine origin and inspiration.

ARTICLE VIII: Human Authors

We affirm that God in His work of inspiration utilized the distinctive personalities and literary styles of the writers whom He had chosen and prepared. We deny that God, in causing these writers to use the very words that He chose, overrode their personalities.

Article VIII reiterates that God's work of inspiration did not cancel out the humanity of the human writers He used to accomplish His purpose. The writers of Scripture were chosen and prepared by God for their sacred task. Whatever the process of inspiration may have been, it did not override their personalities as they wrote. Though it does not say so directly, this article is denying any kind of mechanistic or mechanical inspiration. Mechanical inspiration would reduce the human authors to the level of automatons, robot-like machines. An analysis of Scripture makes clear that the distinctive personalities and writing styles vary from one human writer to another. Luke's style, for example, is obviously different from that of Matthew. The literary structures found in the writing of Daniel differ greatly from those found, for example, in the writing of James. Men of Hebrew origin tended to write in Hebraic styles, and those of the Greek cultural background tended to write in a Greek style. However, God made it possible for His truth to be communicated in an inspired way while making use of the backgrounds, personalities, and literary styles of these various writers. What was overcome or overridden by inspiration was not human personalities, styles, or literary methods, but human tendencies to distortion, falsehood, and error.

Chapter Four

THE BIBLE AND INERRANCY

Articles IX through XII deal with the matter of greatest present concern: inerrancy. They seek to define terms and answer the chief questions that have been raised: If the Bible has come to us through human authors, which the earlier articles acknowledge, and if it is natural for human beings to err, which all confess, isn't the Bible necessarily errant? On the other hand, if it does not have errors, is it still authentically human? Since inerrancy applies properly only to the original manuscripts, the autographs, and since we do not possess these autographs, isn't the argument for inerrancy meaningless? Doesn't it stand only by appealing to documents that do not exist and whose inerrant state cannot be verified? Why can't inerrancy be applied to those parts of the Bible that deal with salvation but not to those parts that deal with history, science, and other "unimportant" and "nonessential" matters?

ARTICLE IX: Inerrancy

We affirm that inspiration, though not conferring omniscience, guaranteed true and trustworthy utterance on all matters of which the biblical authors were moved to speak and write. We deny that the finitude or fallenness of these writers, by necessity or otherwise, introduced distortion or falsehood into God's Word.

The affirmation of Article IX indicates that inspiration guarantees that the writings of Scripture are true and trustworthy. That is, they are not false, deceptive, or fraudulent in what they communicate.

As we dealt with the limitations of human language in Article IV, so we face now the difficulty of the communication of truth by creatures who are not omniscient. It is one thing for God to confer infallibility to the writings and quite another to confer omniscience to the writers. Omniscience and infallibility must be carefully distinguished. Although they are conjoined in God, it is different for man. Omniscience refers to the scope of one's knowledge, while infallibility refers to the reliability of his pronouncements. One who knows better can make a false statement if it is his intention to deceive. Vice versa, a person with limited knowledge can make infallible statements if they can be guaranteed to be completely reliable. Thus, we say that though the biblical writings are inspired, this does not imply that the writers knew everything there was to know or that they were infallible of themselves. The knowledge they communicated is not comprehensive, but it is true and trustworthy as far as it goes.

The denial of Article IX has to do with the writers' likely propensity, as finite and fallen creatures, to introduce distortion or falsehood into God's Word. This issue was covered from another angle in Article IV. But what is in view here is the recurring charge that the teaching of verbal inspiration or a confession of the inerrancy of Scripture carries with it a docetic view of Scripture. Docetism introduced a particular distortion of the biblical view of Jesus. In the earliest days of the Christian church, there were those, usually associated with the school of Gnosticism, who believed that Jesus did not really have a human nature or a human body. They argued that He only appeared to have a physical body. This heresy was called docetism from the Greek word *dokeo*, which means "to seem, to think, or to appear." Those who denied the reality of the incarnation and maintained that Jesus had but a phantom body were accused of this heresy. In a more sophisticated sense, docetism has come to apply to any failure to take seriously the real limitations of the human nature of Jesus.

The charge of biblical docetism has been leveled against advocates of inerrancy, most notably by Karl Barth. He accuses us of holding a view of inspiration in which the true humanity of the biblical writers is canceled out by the intrusion of the divine characteristic of infallibility. For Barth, it is fundamental to our humanity that we are liable to err. If the classic statement is *errare est humanum*, "to err is human," we reply that though this is true, it does not follow that men always err or that error is necessary for humanity. If such were the case, it would be necessary for us to assert that Adam, before he fell, had to err or he was not human. We also would have to assert that in heaven, in a state of glorification, we would have to continue to err if we were to continue to be human. Not only would we have to ascribe error to Adam before the fall and to glorified Christians, we would have to apply it to the incarnate Christ. Error would have been intrinsic to His humanity, so it would have been necessary for Jesus to distort the truth in order to be fully human. Let us never engage in such blasphemy, even though we confess the depth to which we have fallen and our high propensity to err. Even apart from inspiration, it is not necessary for a human being to err in order to be human. So if it is possible for an uninspired person to speak the truth without error, how much more will it be the case for one who is under the influence of inspiration.

Finitude implies a necessary limitation of knowledge but not necessarily a distortion of knowledge. The trustworthy character of the biblical text should not be denied on the ground of man's finitude.

ARTICLE X: The Autographs

*We **affirm** that inspiration, strictly speaking, applies only to the autographic text of Scripture, which in the providence of God can be ascertained from available manuscripts with great accuracy. We further affirm that copies and translations of Scripture are the Word of God to the extent that they faithfully represent the original.*

We deny that any essential element of the Christian faith is affected by the absence of the autographs. We further deny that this absence renders the assertion of biblical inerrancy invalid or irrelevant.

Article X deals directly with the perennial issue of the relationship of the text of Scripture that we now have to the original documents, which have not been preserved except through the means of copies. In the first instance, inspiration applies strictly to the original autographs of Scripture, the original works of the inspired authors. This indicates that the infallible control of God in the production of the original Scriptures has not been perpetuated through the ages in the copying and translating process. It is plainly apparent that there are some minute variations between the manuscript copies that we possess and that the translating process must inject variations for those who read Scripture in a language other than Hebrew and Greek. So the framers of the Chicago Statement are not arguing for a perpetually inspired transmission of the text.

Since we do not have the original manuscripts, some have argued that an appeal to the lost originals renders the whole case for the inspiration of Scripture irrelevant. To reason in this manner is to show contempt for the very serious work that has been done in the field of textual criticism. Textual criticism is the science that seeks to reconstruct an original text by a careful analysis and evaluation of the manuscripts we now possess. This task has to be accomplished with respect to all documents from antiquity that have reached us through manuscript copies. The Old and New Testament Scriptures are probably the texts that have reached us with the most extensive and reliable attestation. For more than ninety-nine percent of the cases, the original text can be reconstructed to a practical certainty. Even in the few cases where some perplexity remains, this does not impinge on the meaning of Scripture to the point of clouding a tenet of the faith or a mandate of life. Thus, in the Bible as we have it (and as it is conveyed to us through faithful translations), we do have, for practical purposes, the very Word of God, inasmuch as the manuscripts convey to us the complete vital truth of the originals.

The further affirmation of Article X is that copies and translations of Scripture are the Word of God to the extent that they faithfully represent the original. Though we do not possess the originals, we have well-reconstructed translations and copies that, to the extent they correspond to the originals, may be said to be the Word of God. But because of the evident presence of copy errors and errors of translation, the distinction must be made between the original work of inspiration in the autographs and the human labor of translating and copying those autographs.

The denial is concerned with the important point that in those minuscule segments of existing manuscripts where textual criticism has not been able to ascertain the original reading with absolute certainty, no essential article of the Christian faith is affected.

To limit inerrancy or inspiration to the original manuscripts does not make the whole contention irrelevant. It does make a difference. If the original text were errant, the church would have the option of rejecting its teachings. If the original text is inerrant (and we must depend on the science of textual criticism to reconstruct that inerrant text), we have no legitimate basis for disobeying a mandate of Scripture where the text is not in doubt. For example, if two theologians agree that the original text was inerrant, and if both agree as to what the present copy teaches and further agree that the present copy is an accurate representation of the original, then it follows irresistibly that the two men are under divine obligation to obey that text. If, on the other hand, we asserted that the original manuscripts were possibly errant, and the two theologians then agreed as to what the Bible taught and also agreed that the present translation or copy faithfully represented the original, neither would be under moral obligation to submit to the teachings of that possibly errant original. Therein lies the importance of the character of the original manuscript.

ARTICLE XI: Infallibility

We affirm that Scripture, having been given by divine inspiration, is infallible, so that, far from misleading us, it is true and reliable in all the matters it addresses. We deny that it is possible for the Bible to be at the same time infallible and errant in its assertions. Infallibility and inerrancy may be distinguished, but not separated.

The central affirmation of Article XI is the infallibility of Scripture. Infallibility is defined in this context in positive terms that imply the truthfulness and reliability of all matters that Scripture addresses. Negatively, infallibility is defined as the quality of that which does not mislead.

The denial of Article XI touches a very important point of controversy, particularly in the modern era. There are those who maintain that the Bible is infallible but not inerrant. Thus, infallibility is separated from inerrancy. The denial argues that it is not possible to maintain with consistency that something is at the same time infallible and errant in its assertions. To maintain such a disjunction between infallibility and inerrancy would involve a glaring contradiction.

Though the words *infallible* and *inerrant* have often been used virtually as synonyms in the English language, there remains a historic technical distinction between the two. The distinction is that of the potential and the actual, the hypothetical and the real. Infallibility has to do with the question of ability or potential; that which is infallible is said to be unable to make mistakes or to err. By contrast, that which is inerrant is that which, in fact, does not err. Theoretically, something may be fallible and at the same time inerrant. That is, it is possible for someone who errs to not err. However, the reverse is not true. If someone is infallible, that means he cannot err, and if he cannot err, then he does not err. If he does err, that proves that he is capable of erring and therefore is not infallible. Thus, to assert that something is infallible yet at the same time errant is to distort the meaning of *infallible* and/or *errant*, or to be in a state of confusion. Infallibility and inerrancy in this sense cannot be separated, though they may be distinguished in terms of meaning.

In situations where the word *infallible* has been substituted for *inerrant*, there usually has been an intent to articulate a lower view of Scripture than that indicated by the word *inerrant*. In fact, however, the term *infallible* in its original and technical meaning is a higher term than *inerrant*. Again, it is important to see that something that is fallible could theoretically be inerrant. But that which is infallible could not theoretically be errant at the same time.

ARTICLE XII: Inerrancy of the Whole

We affirm *that Scripture in its entirety is inerrant, being free from all falsehood, fraud, or deceit.* *We deny* *that biblical infallibility and inerrancy are limited to spiritual, religious, or redemptive themes, exclusive of assertions in the fields of history and science. We further deny that scientific hypotheses about earth history may properly be used to overturn the teaching of Scripture on creation and the flood.*

Article XII asserts clearly and unambiguously the inerrancy of sacred Scripture. In the affirmation, the meaning of inerrancy is given in negative terms: that which is inerrant is "free from all falsehood, fraud, or deceit." Here inerrancy is defined by way of negation, by establishing parameters beyond which we may not move, boundaries we may not transgress. An inerrant Bible cannot contain falsehood, fraud, or deceit in its teachings or assertions.

The denial explicitly rejects the tendency of some to limit infallibility and inerrancy to specific segments of the biblical message, such as spiritual, religious, or redemptive themes, excluding assertions from the fields of history or science. It has been fashionable in certain quarters to maintain that the Bible is not normal history, but is redemptive history, with the accent on the word *redemptive*. Theories are then established that limit inspiration to themes of redemption, allowing the historical dimension to be errant. However, the fact that the Bible is not written like other forms of history does not negate the historical dimension with which it is intimately involved. Though the Bible is indeed *redemptive* history, it is also redemptive *history*, and this means that the acts of salvation wrought by God actually occurred in the space-time world.

With respect to matters of science, the further denial—that scientific hypotheses about earth history may be used to overturn the teaching of Scripture on matters of creation and the flood—again rejects the idea that the Bible speaks authoritatively merely in areas of spiritual value or concerning redemptive themes. The Bible has something to say about the origin of the earth, about the advent of man, and about matters that have scientific import, such as the question of the flood. It is important to note that the second denial does not carry the implication that scientific hypotheses or research are useless to the student of the Bible or that science contributes nothing to an understanding of biblical material. It merely denies that the teaching of Scripture can be overturned by teachings from external sources.

To illustrate the intention of the second denial of Article XII, recall the classic example of the church's debate with the scientific community in the Middle Ages over the question of geocentricity and heliocentricity. The church had adopted the ancient Ptolemaic view that the earth was the center of the universe. Hence, the concept of geocentricity. Scientific inquiry and studies, particularly attending the advent of the telescope, led many scholars to conclude that the sun, not the earth, was the center at least of our solar system; the evidence was compelling and overwhelming. We remember with embarrassment that Galileo was condemned as a heretic for asserting heliocentricity against what the church believed to be the teaching of Scripture. However, the scientific discoveries made it necessary for the church to reexamine the teaching of Scripture to see whether Scripture actually taught geocentricity or whether this was an inference read into the Scripture on the basis of an earlier worldview. Upon reexamining what Scripture really taught, the church came to the conclusion that there was no conflict with science on this question of geocentricity because the Bible did not explicitly teach or assert that the earth was the center of either the solar system or the universe. Here the advance of science helped the church to correct an earlier misinterpretation of Scripture. Thus, to say that science cannot overturn the teaching of Scripture is not to say that science cannot aid the church in understanding Scripture or even correct false inferences drawn from Scripture or actual misinterpretations of Scripture. On the other hand, this view does not give one license to reinterpret Scripture arbitrarily to force it into conformity to secular theories of origins or the like. For example, if the secular community asserts that humanity is the result of a cosmic accident or the product of blind, impersonal forces, such a view cannot possibly be reconciled with the biblical assertion of the purposive act of God's creation of mankind without doing radical violence to the Bible itself.

Questions of biblical interpretation that touch on the field of hermeneutics remain for further investigation and discussion. This article does not spell out what the Scriptures actually teach about creation and the flood, but it does assert that whatever the Bible teaches about creation and the flood cannot be negated by secular theories.

Chapter Five

THE BIBLE
AND TRUTH

The meaning of the word *truth* should be self-evident, but this has not been the case where discussions of the truthfulness of the Bible are concerned. What is truth? Some have argued that the Bible is not truthful unless it conforms to modern standards of scientific precision—no round numbers, precise grammar, scientific descriptions of natural phenomena, and so forth. Others have taken an opposite view, arguing that the Bible is truthful so long as it attains its general spiritual ends, regardless of whether it actually makes false statements. Articles XIII through XV thread their way between these extremes. They maintain that the Bible is to be evaluated by its own principles of truth, which do not necessarily include modern forms of scientific expression, but argue at the same time that the statements of Scripture are always without error and, therefore, do not mislead the reader in any way.

Article XIV deals with the way apparent discrepancies—involving problems not yet resolved—should be handled.

ARTICLE XIII: Truth

We affirm the propriety of using inerrancy as a theological term with reference to the complete truthfulness of Scripture. We deny that it is proper to evaluate Scripture according to standards of truth and error that are alien to its usage or purpose. We further deny that inerrancy is negated by biblical phenomena such as a lack of modern technical precision, irregularities of grammar or spelling, observational descriptions of nature, the reporting of falsehoods, the use of hyperbole and round numbers, the topical arrangement of material, variant selections of material in parallel accounts, or the use of free citations.

It may seem to some, in view of all the qualifications that are listed in the denial of Article XIII, that *inerrancy* is no longer an appropriate term to use with respect to the Bible. Some have said that it has "suffered the death of a thousand qualifications." The same, of course, could be said about the word *God*. Because of the complexity of our concept of God, it has become necessary to qualify in great detail the differences in what is being affirmed and what is being denied when we use the term *God*. Such qualifications do not negate the value of the word but only serve to sharpen its precision and usefulness.

It is important to note that the word *inerrancy* is called a theological term by Article XIII. It is an appropriate theological term to refer to the complete truthfulness of Scripture. That is basically what is being asserted with the term *inerrancy*: that the Bible is completely true, that all its affirmations and denials correspond with reality. Theological terms such as *inerrancy* are frequently in need of qualification and cannot be taken in a crass, literal sense. For example, the term *omnipotence*, when used to refer to God, does not literally mean what it may seem to mean. That is, *omnipotence* does not mean that God can do anything. The fact that God is omnipotent does not mean that He can lie, that He can die, or that He can be God and not God at the same time and in the same relationship. Nevertheless, as a term that has reference to God's complete sovereign control and authority over the created world, *omnipotence* is a perfectly useful and appropriate word in our theological vocabulary.

Because the term *inerrancy* must be qualified, some have thought that it would be better to exclude it from the church's vocabulary. However, the qualifications of the term are not new, nor are they particularly cumbersome, and the word serves as an appropriate safeguard from those who would attack the truthfulness of Scripture in subtle ways. When we speak of inerrancy, then, we are speaking of the fact that the Bible does not violate its own principles of truth. This does not mean that the Bible is free from grammatical irregularities or the like, but that it does not contain assertions that are in conflict with objective reality.

The first denial, that it is proper to evaluate the Bible "according to standards of truth and error that are alien to its usage or purpose," indicates that it would be inappropriate to evaluate the Bible's internal consistency with its own truth claims by standards foreign to its own view of truth. When we say that the truthfulness of Scripture ought to be evaluated according to its own standards, we mean that for Scripture to be true to its claim, it must have an internal consistency compatible with the biblical concept of truth and that all the claims of the Bible must correspond with reality, whether that reality is historical, factual, or spiritual.

The second denial gives us a list of qualifications that is not intended to be exhaustive but rather illustrative of the type of considerations that must be kept in mind when one seeks to define the word *inerrancy*. Let us look at these considerations more closely:

• "Modern technical precision." Inerrancy is not vitiated by the fact, for example, that the Bible occasionally uses round numbers. To say that truth has been distorted when the size of a crowd or the size of an army is estimated in round numbers would be to impose a criterion of truth that is foreign to the literature under examination. Even in modern times, when a news report says that fifty thousand people assembled for a football game, it is not considered to be engaging in falsehood, fraud, or deceit because it has rounded off 49,878 to fifty thousand. This is an appropriate use of quantitative measurement in historical reporting that does not involve falsehood.

• "Irregularities of grammar or spelling." Though it is more beautiful and attractive to speak the truth with a fluent style and proper grammar, grammatical correctness is not necessary for the expression of truth. For example, suppose a man were on trial for murder and was asked whether he killed his wife. If he replied, "I ain't killed nobody never," the crudity of his grammar would have nothing to do with the truth or falsehood of his statement. He could hardly be convicted of murder because his plea of innocence was couched in rough and "errant" grammar. Inerrancy is not related to the grammatical propriety or impropriety of the language of Scripture.

• "Observational descriptions of nature." With respect to natural phenomena, it is clear that the Bible speaks from the perspective of the observer on many occasions. The Bible speaks of the sun rising, moving across the heavens, and setting. From the perspective of common observation, it is perfectly appropriate to describe things as they appear to the human eye. To accuse the Bible of error in describing planetary motion would be to impose a foreign perspective and criterion on the Scriptures. No one is offended when a meteorologist speaks of sunrises and sunsets. No one accuses the National Weather Service of seeking to revert to a medieval perspective of geocentricity by speaking of sunrises and sunsets. Those terms are perfectly appropriate to describe things as they appear to the observer.

• "The reporting of falsehoods." Some have maintained

that the Bible is not inerrant because it reports falsehoods, such as the lies of Satan and the fraudulent teachings of false prophets. However, though the Bible does, in fact, contain false statements, they are reported as being lies and falsehoods. So this in no way vitiates the truth value of the biblical record but only enhances it.

• "The use of hyperbole." Some have appealed to the use of hyperbole as a technical reason for rejecting inerrancy. However, hyperbole is a perfectly legitimate literary device. Hyperbole involves the intentional exaggeration of a statement to make a point. It provides the weight of intensity and emphasis that otherwise would be lacking. That the Bible uses hyperbole is without doubt, but the Chicago Statement denies that hyperbole vitiates inerrancy. The framers of the document maintain that the use of hyperbole is perfectly consistent with the Bible's own view of truth.

Other matters, such as the topical arrangement of material, the use of free citations (for example, from the Old Testament by the New Testament writers), and various selections of material and parallel accounts—where different writers include some information that other writers do not have and delete some information that others include—in no way destroy the truthfulness of what is being reported. Though the biblical writers may have arranged their material differently, they do not affirm that Jesus said on one occasion what He never said on that occasion. Neither do they claim that a parallel account is wrong for not including what they themselves include. As an itinerant preacher, Jesus no doubt said many similar things on different occasions.

Biblical standards of truth and error are those that are used both in the Bible and in everyday life; they have to do with a correspondence view of truth. This part of the article is directed toward those who would redefine truth to relate merely to redemptive intent, the purely personal, or the like, rather than to mean that which corresponds with reality. For example, Jesus affirmed that Jonah was in "the belly of the great fish" (Matt. 12:40), and this statement is true, not simply because of the redemptive significance of the story of Jonah, but also because it is literally and historically true. The same may be said of the New Testament assertions about Adam, Moses, David, and other Old Testament people, as well as about Old Testament events.

ARTICLE XIV: Consistency

*We **affirm** the unity and internal consistency of Scripture. We **deny** that alleged errors and discrepancies that* *have not yet been resolved vitiate the truth claims of the Bible.*

Because the Bible is the Word of God and reflects His truthful character, it is important to affirm that it is one. Though it contains much information of a wide diversity of scope and interest, nevertheless there is an internal unity and consistency to the Word of God that flows from the nature of God's truth. God's truthfulness brings unity out of diversity. God is not an author of incoherency or of contradiction. His Word is consistent as well as coherent.

The denial in Article XIV deals with the particular problems of the harmonization of texts that appear to be contradictory and of other alleged errors and discrepancies pointed out repeatedly by critics. It must be acknowledged that there are some as-yet-unresolved apparent discrepancies in Scripture. A great deal of careful scrutiny has been applied to the investigation of these texts, and that effort has yielded very positive results. A great many alleged contradictions have been resolved, some in the early church and others more recently. The trend has been in the direction of fewer problems rather than more of them. New knowledge about the ancient texts and the meaning of language in the biblical age, as well as new discoveries coming from manuscripts and parchments uncovered by archaeology, have given substantial help in resolving problems and have provided a solid basis for optimism with respect to resolution of remaining difficulties. Difficulties that have not been resolved may yet be resolved under further scrutiny.

This approach to the resolution of difficulties may seem at first glance to be an exercise in "special pleading." However, if any work deserves special consideration, it is sacred Scripture. Before we jump to the conclusion that we are faced with an ultimately unresolvable contradiction, we must exhaust all possible illuminating research. A spirit of humility demands that we give careful attention to the resolutions that already have been made, and that we acknowledge that we have not as yet left no stone unturned in our efforts to give a fair and judicious hearing to the text of the Bible. Some of the greatest discoveries that have helped us to understand the Bible have come about because we have been forced to dig more deeply in our efforts to reconcile difficulties within the text. It should not be deemed strange that a volume that includes sixty-six different books, written over fourteen hundred years, would have some difficulties of harmonization.

It has often been charged that the Bible is *full* of contradictions. Such statements are unwarranted by the evidence. The number of seriously difficult passages compared with the total quantity of material found there is very small indeed. It would be injudicious and even foolhardy for us to ignore the truth claims of the Bible simply because of so-far-unresolved difficulties. We have a parallel here with the presence of anomalies in the scientific world. Anomalies may indeed be so significant that they make it necessary for scientists to rethink their theories about the nature of geology, biology, or the like. For the most part, however, when an overwhelming weight of evidence points to the viability of a theory despite some remaining anomalies that do not seem to fit the theory, it is not the accepted practice in the scientific world to "scrap" the well-attested theory because of a few difficulties that have not yet been resolved. With this analogy in science, we may be bold to say that when we approach Scripture as we do, we do nothing more or less than apply the scientific method to our research of Scripture itself.

Every student of Scripture must face squarely and with honesty the difficulties that are still unresolved. To do this demands our deepest intellectual endeavors. We should seek to learn from Scripture as we examine the text again and again. The unresolved difficulties, in the process of being resolved, often yield light to us as we gain a deeper understanding of the Word of God.

ARTICLE XV: Accommodation

*We **affirm** that the doctrine of inerrancy is grounded in the teaching of the Bible about inspiration. We **deny** that Jesus' teaching about Scripture may be dismissed by appeals to accommodation or to any natural limitation of His humanity.*

In the affirmation of Article XV, inerrancy as a doctrine is viewed as being inseparably related to the biblical teaching on inspiration. Though the Bible nowhere uses the word *inerrancy*, the concept is found in the Scriptures. The Scriptures have their own claim to being the Word of God. The words of the prophets are prefaced by the statement, "Thus says the Lord." Jesus speaks of the Scriptures of the Old Testament as being incapable of being broken (John 10:35). He says that not a jot or tittle of the law will pass away until all is fulfilled (Matt. 5:18). Paul tells us that all is given by inspiration (2 Tim. 3:16). Inerrancy is a corollary of inspiration inasmuch as it is unthinkable that God should inspire that which is fraudulent, false, or deceitful. Thus, though the word *inerrancy* is not explicitly used in the Scriptures, the word *inspiration* is, and the concept of inerrancy is designed to do justice to the concept of inspiration.

It should not be thought that, because the Bible does not contain the terms *inerrant* or *inerrancy,* that there is no biblical basis for the doctrine of inerrancy. The Bible nowhere uses the term *trinity,* and yet the doctrine of the Trinity is clearly taught throughout the New Testament. When the church affirms a doctrine, it finds no necessity to discover a verbal parallel between the doctrine and the words of the Bible itself.

The affirmation of this article implies that the doctrine of the inerrancy of Scripture is a doctrine ultimately based on the teaching of Jesus Himself. The framers of this confession wished to express no higher or lower view of Scripture than that held and taught by Jesus. That becomes explicit in the denial. The denial expresses that Jesus' teaching about Scripture may not be dismissed easily. It has been fashionable for Protestants in recent years to grant that Jesus did indeed hold and teach a doctrine of inspiration that would comport with the concept of inerrancy, but they then argue that Jesus' view was deficient in light of limitations tied to His human nature. The fact that Jesus held a view of inspiration such as He did is "excused" on the basis that, touching His human nature, Jesus was a product of His times. Jesus, it is said, could not possibly have known all of the problems that have since been raised by higher criticism. As a result, Jesus, like the rest of His contemporaries, accepted uncritically the prevailing notion of Scripture of His own day. For example, it is said that when Jesus mentioned that Moses wrote of Him, He was unaware of the documentary hypothesis that apparently demolishes any serious case for Mosaic authorship of the first five books of the Old Testament.

Such supposed ignorance by Jesus concerning the truth about Scripture is excused by the argument that He could have known the truth only if He was omniscient in His human nature. For Jesus to have been omniscient in His human nature, that is, to have known all things, would have involved a confusion of the divine and human natures. Omniscience is an attribute of deity, not of humanity. Since Protestants ordinarily do not believe that Jesus' human nature was deified with such attributes as omniscience, it appears perfectly understandable and excusable that in His lack of knowledge He made mistakes about Scripture. This is the line of reasoning that the denial disallows.

The problems raised by these explanations are too numerous and too profound for a detailed treatment here. But even though we admit that Jesus was not omniscient in His human nature, we assert that His claims to teach nothing by His own authority but by the authority of the Father (John 8:28) and to be the very incarnation of truth

(John 14:6) would be fraudulent if He taught anything in error. Even if He made an error arising out of ignorance, He would be guilty of sin for claiming to know truth that He in fact did not know. At stake here is our very redemption. If Jesus taught falsely while claiming to be speaking the truth, He was guilty of sin. If He was guilty of sin, His atonement could not atone for Himself, let alone for His people. Ultimately, the doctrine of Scripture is bound up with the doctrine of Jesus Christ. It is because of Jesus' high view of Scripture that the framers of this confession so strenuously maintain a high view of Scripture today.

Again, it is fashionable in many circles to believe Jesus when He speaks of heavenly matters, matters of redemption and salvation, but to correct Him when He speaks of historical matters such as the writing of the Pentateuch and other matters relating to the doctrine of Scripture. At this point, those who accept Jesus when He speaks redemptively but reject Him when He speaks historically violate a teaching principle that Jesus Himself espoused. Jesus raised the rhetorical question, "If I have told you earthly things and you do not believe, how can you believe if I tell you heavenly things?" (John 3:12). It seems that we have a generation of scholars who are willing to believe Jesus concerning heavenly matters while rejecting those things that He taught about the earth. (What Jesus says concerning history may be falsified by critical methods, but what He says concerning heavenly matters is beyond the reach of verification of falsification.) The framers of this confession believe that Jesus' principle of the trustworthiness of His teaching as affecting both heavenly matters and earthly matters must be maintained even to this day.

Chapter Six

THE BIBLE
AND YOU

Discussion of inerrancy is merely an academic exercise unless it concerns the individual Christian on the level of his growth in God. This is precisely what it does. Confession of the full authority and inerrancy of Scripture should lead us to increasing conformity to the image of Christ, which is the God-ordained goal of every Christian. The final Articles of Affirmation and Denial in the Chicago Statement deal with this matter.

ARTICLE XVI: Church History

*We **affirm** that the doctrine of inerrancy has been integral to the church's faith throughout its history. We **deny** that inerrancy is a doctrine invented by scholastic Protestantism, or is a reactionary position postulated in response to negative higher criticism.*

This affirmation again speaks of the doctrine of inerrancy, not the word *inerrancy*. It is readily acknowledged that the word *inerrancy* was not used with any degree of frequency and perhaps not even at all before the seventeenth century. For example, Martin Luther nowhere uses the term *inerrancy* as a noun with respect to Scripture. Because of this, some have said that Luther did not believe in inerrancy. However, Luther argued that the Scriptures never "err." To say that the Scriptures never err is to say nothing more or less than that the Bible is inerrant. So though the word *inerrancy* is of relatively modern invention, the concept is rooted not only in the biblical witness to Scripture itself but also in its acceptance by the vast majority of God's people throughout the history of the Christian church. We find the doctrine taught, embraced and espoused by men such as Augustine, Thomas Aquinas, John Calvin, Jonathan Edwards, and other Christian scholars and teachers throughout church history. While the language of inerrancy does not appear in Protestant confessions of faith until the modern ages, the concept of inerrancy is surely not foreign or strange to the confessions of East or West, Catholic or Protestant.

The denial follows the thinking of the affirmation closely. It states that inerrancy as a concept is not the product of a rigid, sterile, rationalistic approach to Scripture born of the scholastic movement of seventeenth-century Protestantism. Neither is it proper to understand the doctrine as a twentieth-century reaction to liberal theology or "modernism."

It is not the affirmation of inerrancy that is of recent vintage; it is its denial. It is not the reaction to higher criticism that is new; it is the appearance of philosophical assumptions of negative criticism. Such criticism is not new in the sense that no one ever questioned the integrity or authenticity of Scripture in past ages, but the newness of the phenomenon is its widespread and easy acceptance within churches and by leaders who would claim allegiance to mainline Christianity.

ARTICLE XVII: Witness of the Spirit

*We **affirm** that the Holy Spirit bears witness to the Scriptures, assuring believers of the truthfulness of God's* *written Word.* **We deny** *that this witness of the Holy Spirit operates in isolation from or against Scripture.*

Article XVII attests to the doctrine of the internal testimony of the Holy Spirit. That is to say, our personal conviction of the truth of Scripture rests not on the external evidences to Scripture's truthfulness in and of themselves, but those evidences are confirmed in our hearts by the special work of God the Holy Spirit. The Spirit Himself bears witness to our human spirits that the Scriptures are indeed the Word of God. Here God Himself confirms the truthfulness of His own Word.

The denial guards against substituting a reliance on the immediate guidance of the Holy Spirit for the content of Scripture itself. The thought behind the denial is that the Holy Spirit normally works in conjunction with Scripture and speaks to us through Scripture, not against Scripture or apart from Scripture. Word and Spirit are to be viewed together, Word bearing witness to the Spirit and being the means by which we test the spirits to see if they be of God (1 John 4:1), and the Spirit working in our hearts to confirm the Word of God to us. Thus, there is reciprocity between Word and Spirit, and they are never to be set over against each other.

ARTICLE XVIII: Interpretation

*We **affirm** that the text of Scripture is to be interpreted by grammatico-historical exegesis, taking account of its literary forms and devices, and that Scripture is to interpret Scripture. We **deny** the legitimacy of any treatment of the text or quest for sources lying behind it that leads to relativizing, dehistoricizing, or discounting its teaching, or rejecting its claims to authorship.*

Article XVIII touches on some of the most basic principles of biblical interpretation. Though this article does not spell out in detail a comprehensive system of hermeneutics, it gives basic guidelines on which the framers of the confession were able to agree. The first is that the text of Scripture is to be interpreted by grammatico-historical exegesis. *Grammatico-historical* is a term that refers to the process by which we take the structures and time periods of the texts seriously as we interpret them. Biblical interpreters are not given the license to spiritualize or allegorize a text against the grammatical structure and form of the text itself. The Bible is not to be reinterpreted to be brought into conformity with contemporary philosophies but is to be understood in its intended meaning and word usage as it was written at the time it was composed. To hold to grammatico-historical exegesis is to disallow the Bible to be shaped and reshaped according to modern conventions of thought.

The second principle of the affirmation is that we are to take account of the literary forms and devices that are found within the Scriptures themselves. This goes back to principles of interpretation espoused by Luther and the Reformers. A verb is to be interpreted as a verb, a noun as a noun, a parable as a parable, didactic literature as didactic literature, poetry as poetry, and the like. To turn narrative history into poetry or poetry into narrative history would be to violate the intended meaning of the text. Thus, it is important for all biblical interpreters to be aware of the literary forms and grammatical structures that are found within Scripture. An analysis of these forms is proper and appropriate for any correct interpretation of the text.

The third principle in the affirmation is that Scripture is to interpret Scripture. It rests on the previous affirmation that the Bible represents a unified, consistent, and coherent Word from God. Any interpretation of a passage that yields a meaning in direct contradiction to another portion of Scripture is disallowed. It is when Scripture interprets Scripture that the sovereignty of the Holy Spirit, the supreme interpreter of the Bible, is duly acknowledged. Arbitrarily setting one part of

Scripture against another would violate this principle. Scripture is to be interpreted not only in terms of its immediate context but also of the whole context of the Word of God.

The denial of Article XVIII decries the propriety of critical analyses of the text that produce a relativization of the Bible. This does not prohibit an appropriate quest for literary sources or even oral sources that may be discerned through source criticism, but it draws a line as to the extent to which such critical analysis can go. When the quest for sources produces a dehistoricizing of the Bible, a rejection of its teaching, or a rejection of the Bible's own claims of authorship, it has trespassed beyond its proper limits. This does not prohibit the external examination of evidence to discover the unstated authorship of books in sacred Scripture, such as the epistle to the Hebrews. A search is even allowable for literary traditions that may have been brought together by a final editor whose name is mentioned in Scripture. It is never legitimate, however, to run counter to express biblical affirmations.

ARTICLE XIX: Health of the Church

We affirm that a confession of the full authority, infallibility, and inerrancy of Scripture is vital to a sound *understanding of the whole of the Christian faith. We further affirm that such confession should lead to increasing conformity to the image of Christ. **We deny** that such confession is necessary for salvation. However, we further deny that inerrancy can be rejected without grave consequences, both to the individual and to the church.*

Article XIX's affirmation speaks to the relevance of the doctrine of inerrancy to the life of the Christian. Here the functional character of biblical authority is in view. The article is affirming that the confession is not limited to doctrinal concern for theological purity but originates in a profound concern that the Bible remain the authority for living out the Christian life. It also recognizes that it is possible for people to believe in the inerrancy or infallibility of Scripture and lead godless lives. It recognizes that a confession of a doctrine of Scripture is not enough to bring us to sanctification, but that it is a very important part of the growth process of the Christian to rest his confidence in the truthful revelation of the Word of God and thereby be moved inwardly to conform to the image of Christ. A strong doctrine of the authority of Scripture, when properly implemented, should lead a person to a greater degree of conformity to that Word he espouses as true.

The denial in Article XIX is very important. The framers of the confession are saying unambiguously that confession of belief in the inerrancy of Scripture is not an element of the Christian faith essential for salvation. We gladly acknowledge that people who do not hold to this doctrine may be earnest, genuine, zealous, and in many ways dedicated Christians. We do not regard acceptance of inerrancy to be a test for salvation. However, the framers urge people to consider the severe consequences that may befall the individual or church that casually and easily rejects inerrancy. We believe that history has demonstrated again and again that all too often there is a close relationship between rejection of inerrancy and subsequent defections from matters of the Christian faith that are essential to salvation. When the church loses its confidence in the authority of sacred Scripture, it inevitably looks to human opinion as its guiding light. When that happens, the purity of the church is direly threatened.

Thus, we urge our Christian brothers and sisters of all professions and denominations to join with us in a reaffirmation of the full authority, integrity, infallibility, and inerrancy of sacred Scripture, to the end that our lives may be brought under the authority of God's Word, that we may glorify Christ individually and corporately as the church.

About the Author

Dr. R. C. Sproul is the founder and chairman of Ligonier Ministries, an international multimedia ministry based in Sanford, Florida. He also serves as senior minister of preaching and teaching at Saint Andrew's, a Reformed congregation in Sanford, and as president of Reformation Bible College, and his teaching can be heard around the world on the daily radio program *Renewing Your Mind*.

During his distinguished academic career, Dr. Sproul helped train men for the ministry as a professor at several theological seminaries.

He is the author of more than eighty books, including *The Holiness of God*, *Chosen by God*, *The Invisible Hand*, *Faith Alone*, *A Taste of Heaven*, *Truths We Confess*, *The Truth of the Cross*, and *The Prayer of the Lord*. He also served as general editor of *The Reformation Study Bible* and has written several children's books, including *The Prince's Poison Cup*.

Dr. Sproul and his wife, Vesta, make their home in Longwood, Florida.

Further your Bible study with *Tabletalk* magazine, another learning tool from R.C. Sproul.

....

TABLETALK MAGAZINE FEATURES:

A Bible study for each day—Bringing the best in biblical scholarship together with down-to-earth writing, *Tabletalk* helps you understand the Bible and apply it to daily living.

Trusted theological resource—*Tabletalk* avoids trends, shallow doctrine and popular movements to present biblical truth simply and clearly.

Corresponding digital edition—Print subscribers have access to the digital edition for iPad, Kindle Fire, and Android tablet devices.

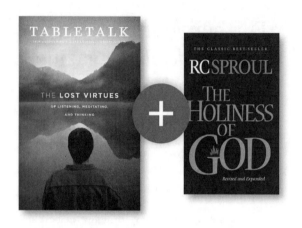

Sign-up for a free, 3-month trial
of *Tabletalk* magazine
and get *The Holiness of God*
by R.C. Sproul for free.

Go online at TryTabletalk.com/CQ